P A T R I C I A   K I R W I N

A Universe Unto Itself

To order additional copies of this book, contact:
Xlibris Corporation
1-888-795-4274
www.Xlibris.com
Orders@Xlibris.com
100562

DEDICATION TO MY LOVED ONES

I wish you calm seas,

Blue skies,

Flowers in springtime,

And a heart full of love

Until forever is just another day

Patricia Kirwin August 6, 2011

To my children and grandchildren

THE HOUR GLASS

Millions of years have passed since the first brimming of the Earth's hour glass occurred.

Billions of souls have disappeared, a few slipped down into the bottle neck and survived. How many ice ages have happened and where are the burial grounds?

Millions of years ago, were there civilizations as advanced as we are today? Did they clone and murder their offspring at very nearly the same rate?

Our accomplishments are magnificent. Our power awesome, but what good will that do when the hour glass fills once again, and who will be left to go forth and replenish the earth? Scientific theory has it that all DNA found present on Earth today in billions of cells slipped through the hour glass during prehistoric times.

A UNIVERSE UNTO ITSELF

And from the vast depth of infinity there came forth a universe that was unto itself wondrous, for out of that macrocosm there emerged earth, the most beauteous and omnipotent planet of them all.

Deep within its seas another universe evolved and creatures by the millions began to thrive and in time the first cell of a brain was formed. Many millenniums passed before a complete brain was developed and that very brain was a universe unto itself.

Some creatures crawled up onto the land and as their brains continued to develop each was in itself unique.

Ten millenniums passed and the heavens were at peace and the earth was beautiful. Many species existed. Each in its' turn conquered and ruled the planet. The largest of all reigned for one hundred and forty million years.

Magnificent creatures great and small came and left the environment, each having served its' own purpose. In time, a special animal emerged and soon he walked erect, for his evolution was very nearly complete. His reign was just beginning and the universe of his brain was awesome, for therein were contained the star cells of memory. This one who walked erect commanded the other animals, who had brains of an inferior universe. And this creature walked the earth for ten thousand more years, until there came forth that animating and vital principal of its' species credited with thought, action, and emotion. A mind coexisting with its' body that was able to think and wonder.

The universe of every human brain continued to increase naturally by the assimilation of memory and accretion so that the memory cells of each cranial universe contained the genetic memory of all ancestors going back to the first woman.

Therefore, after man had in this way come to be, all men had within recollection of every memory of each ancestor who had gone before him. In this way, for a time, mankind was full of pure wisdom without the necessity of experience and it was through this pure, primitive wisdom that humanity survived upon earth as was the plan.

This channeling of memory from all human ancestors has not vanished as many believe. Memory must be drawn upon. Perhaps, as verbalization replaced telepathic communication, genetic memory was gradually clouded in much the same way that a newborn blindfolded from birth will become blind in spite of having formed eyes. On the other hand, a healthy, mature newborn will make swimming motions if placed in warm water, take steps putting one foot in front of the other if held in an upright position with toes touching the ground, and grasp firmly in fear of falling. Is this not genetic memory?

And just as the newborn loses some of these instincts soon after birth and must be retaught, can adults not also be taught that we too somehow can find the key to unlocking our memory bank, not only of childhood experiences, but the very memories of our ancestors going back into time. Is this not true immortality?

I believe the gift is within reach of all of us and ...

That is why today from sea to sea there are those who possess the gift of channeling and it is called; "Phenomenon".

North America claims many people all of whom are phenomenal. They are called autistic savants for they are geniuses, yet severely challenged. Their creative genius manifests itself in science, mathematics, art and sculpture.

They are exquisitely precious, for their gift is a pure channeling of Godliness. Still, in prehistoric life nothing was phenomenal only natural and the magnificence of the human brain was pure and that which distinguished it from the animals was its' ability to "Wonder".

Therefore, every human creature to come about through mitosis is unto itself a universe in a most powerful galaxy, and the center of each universe is also a universe unto itself and is called the brain, and every human brain is unique with its' ancestral memory.

GENETIC MEMORY

I associate the theory of genetic memory with Deja Vue or the illusion of having already experienced something that is actually happening for the first time. Such experiences date back into the mist of prehistory and many believe that the widespread belief in reincarnation was born of this phenomenon. Surely ancient, medieval and even primitive tribes give credence through their rituals to "the experience".

Though I do not have "the elegance of mind" to understand the gift, I can only say that when I experience the memory I am filled with joy and the feeling of being loved. It comes from within and from out of the past and I am at peace.

Patricia Kirwin Renaud

THE MEMORY OF THE
JUST IS BLESSED

Proverbs 10: 7

For in the galaxy of love there must exist memory. Simple, biologic, genetic, and Divine.

Simple memory is the faculty of retaining and recalling past experiences or the ability to remember.

Biological memory is the persistent modification of behavior resulting from an organism's experience.

Genetic Memory is the memory locked deep within the first brain cell's potential at the moment of conception. For every brain contains the memory cells of every ancestor going back to the first woman.

Divine memory is that which is God's. "For whilst you were still within thine own mother's womb I knew Thee."

Holy Scripture

LOVE IS FROM MEMORY

"For the greatest commandment of all is Love....Love God...

...Love thy neighbor...
...Love Thyself..."

Holy Scripture.... Jesus of Nazareth....

"And during the end times I will pour forth my knowledge upon the earth"

Revelations...

"Go Ye therefore and replenish the earth" ....Genesis....

Scientists believe that the earth has endured ten ice ages during the last one million years. Some believe that another ice age will come within the next ten thousand years.

"And heaven and earth shall all pass away but my word will not pass away"...

Holy Scripture...Jesus of Nazareth....

Heaven according to Webster is a place or state of supreme happiness, a thing or place which is wonderful or enchantingly perfect. Was the world once this way before darkness entombed it in ice?

Why does scripture use the word "replenish" the earth? Replenish means to fill again that which has been full once before.

I am filled with fascination about the ice ages and the darkness that fell over the the world. I conjure up thoughts of toppling glaciers that crushed the earth's structures into mounds of powder.

I wonder why carbon is layered in today's existing glaciers the way it is and what gasses were produced on earth ten million years ago?

Did Jesus know? What did He mean? Heaven and earth will all pass away? Was the heaven He referred to a state of supreme happiness that the earth once knew and will know once again before it shall all pass away? Was Jesus talking about earth in a general sense or was He talking about each one of us who abides upon earth? Are we not each one a universe unto ourselves with millions of star cells in our very own galaxy? Was His Memory divine?

MEMORY THAT IS MY VERY OWN

The most powerful element in the galaxy is memory.

In the universe that is Me. Though I have come about through mitosis, or the sequential differation of replicated chromosomes in a cell nucleus that completes cell division, memory is infused into the universe of my brain through spiritual absorption. In this way, though I can only inherit the colour of my eyes or length of my bones through direct ancestral sequence, I can inherit genetic memory from every experience, word, or action taken in by all in my ancestral line.

Though Mother Teresa is childless, her words and blessed works have spread across India and the entire world. They, therefore, have been absorbed through spiritual infusion into the memory cells of millions and will be passed down to their descendants. In this way Mother Teresa is a true descendant of Jesus or child of God.

"Therefore, I say unto you that heaven and earth will all pass away, but my word will not pass away." Contained in the universe of my brain are the cells of genetic memory to be carried on forever.

DIVINE MEMORY

The God of my universe is my God. It is inanimate. It is the omnipotent power. It is the power of love. It is the power of goodness infused into my being. Only through God, or that which is goodness, can my universe attain harmony in the galaxy.

The endless search for love is goodness. So often have I grasped it, so many times have I lost it. I have seen many dawns now, many glorious sunsets, and still I search and hope. Never will I despair, for I know that each temptation resisted, every prayer answered, is of love, the greatest commandment of them all. I know that my God of goodness is love, for it is the power that is God.

To accuse one of being self-absorbed seems to be harsh criticism, and yet, without it my universe cannot survive, for if one cell planet is out of line or off course it can mean the destruction of the spilling galaxy of life.

Therefore, one must be self-absorbed, it is essential to survival, as important as the recognition of that very need in others.

For every trespass against others will harm my universe, far more than those transgressions against it.

That is why when I hurt others my own wound is deep, even as I search for my God.

THE GIFT OF CHOICE

The Gift Of Choice

I gave you springtime.

You cried because it rained.

I gave you warmth in summertime.

But the heat brought you discomfort.

I gave you glorious autumn.

And you fretted for winters' coming.

I gave you winter.

And you died in the cold.

I gave her darkness.

She rejoiced in a sunbeam.

I gave her drought.

Yet she hoped for the harvest.

I gave her autumn and she fell in love

with its' beauty.

I gave her winter and she fell asleep

in my arms.

Patricia Kirwin

Chapter I

IN THE BEGINNING

How Many Are Your Works, Oh Lord!

In Wisdom You Have Made Them All.

Psalm 104: 24

For millions of millenniums have come and passed and many times has the earth hovered in darkness and ice, but always it has been replenished by the light.

Go Ye Therefore and replenish the earth.

FOR THE FIRST TIME

CHAPTER I

Twilight was wondrous on the eve of their first meeting. Pastel prisms spilled down from the sky and fell in a delicate spray over the clear water below. Along the shoreline, puffs of sea foam danced like tumbleweeds in the soft summer breeze. The earth's sounds were melodious and peaceful.

The sun descended reluctantly as though not wanting to miss the performance of its' own creation. Colors swelled up from the water and fell down from the skies, until in a vibrant crescendo, the earth was enveloped in the radiant hues of a rainbow. Liquid evening slipped in gradually in a mist of midnight blue and the sky was clear save for a full silver moon.

Her smile was shy, so as not to reveal the wild beating of her excited heart. He was taller but surely of the same species. Neither had ever before seen one in his own image and likeness.

Summer's fragrance wafted through the moist night air and heaven fell gently upon them.

He reached out first. They could not make sounds as could the other animals for they were mute, but knowing no other way, they were content. They smiled and touched and absorbed and this was the beginning of their adoration. One for the other.

They were different in one way and this caused them puzzlement at first, until she smiled and pointed to a pair of little rabbits, mating in the moonlight. He smiled and at that moment they understood their nature and had deep respect for their difference and were full of awe. Thereafter, during every twilight they remembered their first meeting and saw very clearly one another's thoughts. Forevermore, every shared experience was stored in the cells of their brains, until at all times they could visualize clearly the thoughts of one another, even when they were separated by distance.

They had many children and all were born with the memory of their parents' first meeting, stored safely in their brain cells, as was every other experience of their parents. For it was natural.

And during seven hundred millenniums they evolved naturally and peace reigned, for they were gentle gatherers, and the fruits of the land were plentiful for their bounty. They knew not hatred nor jealousy. They consummated their love and shared equally, without envy, the products of their conception, which were in every way whole and perfect.

Love was lost gradually when darkness fell over the earth, for the spirit that came was not of goodness, and soon every seed was contaminated. In time, that which was pure and natural was lost, innocence was betrayed, and kindliness for one another slowly evaporated.

During the next five millenniums, great progress was made, great leaps in erotic evolution, and desire accompanied scientific discoveries of all kind, so no longer were the innocent gatherers dominant, but rather the hunters of both good and evil, and each in its' turn prevailed.

In time, life on the planet was at once wondrous and fearful, awesome, and awful. It was a time of greatness and a time of defeat.

Communication to all parts of the planet was immediate through technology that was comprehensible to only the most intellectually elite. While at the same time all were able to take advantage of the very latest, scientific discoveries in science, medicine, and engineering. Inter-planetary trips were frequent and the discoveries there awesome. Most inspiring of all was the discovery of heaven before death.

All disease and deformity of body and mind was eradicated through genetic selection. And virus' remained dormant.

The earth knew a millennium of peace, when war was of the past and too horrendous to contemplate. Neither love not hate prevailed, though acceptance of all was universal. People spoke of their heaven upon earth and life immortal without death. All worshipped immortality and the intelligence of the New World Order. And during this period, before the frozen water vapors descended over the earth, to cast it beneath the ice, the good were transported safely, in a rapturous ascent into the heavens above.

Those left suffered great travail before succumbing to the darkness and endless frost. For they were the malcontents who would not understand the beauty of life nor the gift of holy enchantment. For they were doomed, by their own choice, to lives of misery without regard for the very gift of life.

AND THERE CAME THEREFORE
A REPLENISHING IN THE EAST
THAT WAS AT FIRST
WONDERFUL

CHAPTER ONE
BEFORE DARKNESS

In the distance, he could see the white domes of Balavar glistening in the morning sun. They could reach the river bed by sunset. He thought of Sara, and a rush of pleasure surged through his being.

He stared into the blue emptiness above and for the moment became part of it.

"She is only a slave," the words echoed in his mind.

"Then I, too, am a slave," Kareem whispered.

He sipped the last of his water and called for his servant. A young lad brought in a silver container and filled a large porcelain jug to capacity.

"Have we plenty to spare?" the prince asked him.

"We have nearly two vats, sire."

Kareem dismissed the lad, poured half of the precious liquid into a basin, and began to swill his face and hands.

The caravan moved along slowly. The hot, yellow sun showed no mercy. Shimmering, blue lakes appeared to mock them and then vanished in the sand as they approached.

It was near day's end when the wet, clopping sounds of the slaves pounding their master's garments with stones echoed softly over the dunes and reached the caravan. Kareem let the melody mesmerize him. They were not far now.

"Tomorrow," he whispered.

He thought of the aesthetic movements of Sara's naked body bathing in the cool water near the river's edge. He saw her emerge, slip into the white sari she had carelessly dropped on the bank and walk slowly away.

His dream ended with the sound of men approaching. His host had sent them to accompany him to his home. Joacim seemed more enthusiastic about the reunion than did the prince.

Gold statues stood guard at intervals along the white, marble corridor leading to the atrium where a lady was waiting. In the center of the room, a magnificent fountain splashed over its sculptures into a mosaic basin made of precious stones. Tapestries of cobalt and rose color depicting the emergence of Balavar adorned every wall.

The lady bowed deeply as the prince approached her.

"This is Ellana," Joacim said, the pride in his eyes betrayed the casualness of his tone.

"As always your lady is beautiful," Kareem said, sensing the affection between the two of them.

The lady did not speak, but exchanged glances with both men that said "I am your equal."

"May I call you Ellana, then?" Kareem asked.

And with that unspoken permission to speak before the prince given, she replied, "Yes sir, that is my name."

Kareem smiled.

She left then and walked out into the courtyard alone. A servant brought them wine and fruit. Kareem was seated before Joacim took his place facing him.

"It has been too long," the older one said. "How is your father?"

"He sleeps well, now that Elias is finished," Kareem shrugged indifferently.

"Ah, yes! Your father suffered much because of him."

"He misses him, I think. They became friends, you know, before the end."

"The execution, you mean."

"Yes."

"He should not grieve. These things must be."

"He was his brother."

"Still, he would have killed him sooner or later."

"I am glad I have no brother to hate me."

"Let us speak of the mission . . . the talisman."

"It must be presented during the eclipse."

"Tomorrow, then."

"Tomorrow."

"Good night, your highness."

"Good night, Joacim."

The morning's heat was oppressive. By mid-day, even the slaves had found shelter in the cool, damp crevices within the walls of the city.

Sara could not be found; moreover, all eyes filled with terror at the very mention of her name. Kareem suspected malicious trickery. It was not above the nature of his father. He returned to the palace. Joacim was seated in the courtyard with his lady while a servant ministered to them.

"You need to abide by your father's will, Kareem," Joacim spoke first.

"Where is she?"

"I do not know."

"Do you not rule in Balavar?"

"I do not know," Joacim repeated.

"My father has taken your will completely then."

"He is my friend."

"You are his subject!"

"Yes."

"Remember that one day I will be king!"

"She is not in harm's way," the woman spoke out.

"You know, then?" Kareem's eyes blackened.

"Only that she is safe with Fileece."

"And you!" Kareem glared at Joacim.

"You dare to beg for the talisman."

Joacim grew pale and was silent.

"Will you have your men kill me for it, Joacim? Do you invite my father's wrath over my death?"

"There will be no murder in Balavar," Joacim raised his voice, but he was trembling.

"If the talisman leaves with you tomorrow, so be it."

"I am being evicted then?"

"You are the son of a king; my home is yours."

"I will find Sara without you."

"Perhaps it is just."

"Will you not tell me that it is unnatural to bring a slave into our immaculate caste of kings?"

"It is said that it is unnatural."

"Perhaps it is," Kareem said, "for I would bring innocence and purity into malignant fear and depravity. Into a caste that murders its own in anger and then grieves in loneliness and self-hatred."

"My father believes it is unnatural to unite with slaves; yet, she is wild, magnificent, unspoiled, and perfect in every way. My father believes she would soil our heritage for generations to come. In fact, she is our only hope."

"My home is yours, Kareem," Joacim repeated. "Be comfortable here." The other two arose together and left him alone in the courtyard.

The next day brought him no comfort. No one knew of Sara, save a simple, old woman who babbled about paradise.

"She is daft," the others said. "Be merciful, Lord."

"You will find her near Aravon," the old one said. "She is with Fileece."

Kareem's heart leapt beneath his vestment. "Old woman! I beg of you," he began, but she only stared off into space and resumed her babbling in a foreign tongue that none understood.

"See that she is taken care of," Kareem demanded of Jama Maraan, the son of his mother's ayah who travelled with him.

The fountain at Joacim's palace was magnificent during twilight that night. With every stage of sunset, the colourant variation was more splendid than the last. Spraying mist changed from violet to rose and then gold as the last sunbeams danced on the falling water.

"Water soothes the soul," Jama said, coming closer to the prince. "See how it splashes so softly over the marble?"

"She is so like this," Kareem thought. "She loves this time of day, meditation time, she calls it."

"Why do we worship?" he had asked her once.

"It brings consolation," she had replied.

"Why then do we glorify?"

"For self-glorification," she said without pause.

"I need you, Sara."

. . . .

Joacim placed the talisman in a gold tabernacle. The whole business troubled Jama.

"I do not want it," Kareem asserted. "It is a part of my family that I chose to depart from. It is dark. I don't like it."

"During the eclipse today, two esteemed astrologers were blinded, yet no animal in Balavar was affected."

"Perhaps that is because the dogs are much wiser," Jama chided. "They did not look up as did the other fools."

Night had fallen by the time Kareem entered his chambers. A sliver of silver light trickled through the ceiling window and onto the bedstead. As he turned, he saw the figure of a woman standing across the room. Her hair caught the glow of evening and shone like gold threads in the moonlight.

He gasped as the figure moved slowly towards him. She wore robes of woven silk that fell like soft, white petals over her slender frame.

The enchantment was everywhere. The room became illuminated as the figure moved ever closer. "The talisman," Kareem whispered.

The sound of her sobs broke the spell.

All was still for some time before Kareem broke the silence. "You . . . You are but a child," Kareem said with puzzlement. "Why?"

"I am sent to be yours, my prince." the girl whispered.

"You may stay here, little one. You are safe. Don't cry now. I will not take you. I will not harm you, child."

The prince closed the door softly and stormed into the garden.

"Jama!" he bellowed. "Find Joacim."

"I am here," came a voice.

"What is this?"

"I see that I have made a mistake in judgment. I beg your forgiveness, Kareem."

"Mistake!!! I am beyond anger with you."

"Please, my prince, the mistake is mine," Ellana cried from the shadow. "I only thought to please and distract you."

"How dare you! Have you no compassion? You are a woman."

The prince held back and contained himself. "It is the talisman," he said to Jama.

"You see its evil presence has already contaminated this house, and you wonder why I want no part of it."

When Kareem returned to his suite, the girl was curled up on a mat near the door fast asleep. She is so young, Kareem thought, what evil lurks out there for her; what evil lurks behind these walls for her?

"Awaken, child" he said softly. Her eyes, when widened in fright, were remarkably like Sara's.

"What is your name, sleepy one?" Kareem smiled down at the trembling girl.

"Alleecia," she could barely whisper.

"How old are you?"

"I have completed twelve years."

"Do you know who I am?"

"Yes, prince."

"Do you know why you have been offered to me?"

"They say I am like Sara?"

"Ah!, You know then."

"Yes, your highness."

"Do you know where Sara is?"

The girl's eyes widened once more and became the more enchanting.

"You look like a frightened rabbit," Kareem smiled, "Are you afraid of me?"

"No, sir . . . yes, sir . . . I . . ."

"No, sir; yes, sir; yes, prince; no prince," Kareem's voice was gentle and fatherly. He smiled and took both her hands into his own.

"You may stand," he said gently pulling her to her feet. She was taller than he expected and still trembling. Her delicate hands were cold as ice, and he could see that she was trying hard not to cry, but her lower lip was quivering out of control.

"Alleecia, I will not harm you," Kareem tried to comfort.

"I have not been . . . with . . . I am . . ."

"A virgin."

"Yes, prince."

Kareem smiled again. "I know that Alleecia. Only a virgin can be sacrificed to a prince. Do you know how evil I believe that is?"

"No, sir."

"Your hands are cold and you are trembling. Come let me wrap you in this garment of lamb's wool. When you have regained your composure, we will speak of my plan."

The next day, Alleecia cowered and catered to Kareem's every wish, following him at a distance of two paces. She looked radiant with happiness, but Kareem barely acknowledged her presence, that is unless she left his side for private reasons. Then he would enquire of her whereabouts from at least three servants.

All the wise people smiled about their own wisdom. All save Ellana who was wiser than the rest.

That night, Kareem and Alleecia slipped out alone.

Sara was imprisoned in a small abode in a rural district Northeast of Balavar. The capo was an ancient one said to be very wise.

"I'll take you home first," Kareem said to Alleecia. "Don't be afraid. You have done well, and you will be rewarded."

"It is only that my family. . ."

"Your family will be protected. Don't you trust me, Alleecia?" You must trust me."

"I do, sire."

No one spoke when Kareem entered with Alleecia. All eyes darted from the prince to the girl and then one another. Alleecia bowed to her father and mother, but they did not move to embrace her.

"I am the Prince Mahra Kareem of Judar," Kareem said with humility. "I return your daughter safe and whole unto your family once more."

No one spoke for it seemed an endless moment. Kareem feared the worst, that is that his compassion would be construed as princely rejection and that Alleecia would be marked forever. The silence grew stronger.

"I am Marcus, her father," the words resounded clearly. "I offer my life to you in payment." The prince smiled upon the man and blessed his home.

"Continue to walk in the ways of our God and fear not, Marcus, for evil shall not disrupt your home again."

Sara was radiant. The garden behind her took on the glow of moonlight with every whisper of its closing flowers.

"I knew you would come," she said. She smiled, but did not approach him. As always, she was submissive to his royal standard.

"Come here, Sara." he implored more than commanded, and when she did, all was the same. All was now and everlasting as though they had never parted. Their souls were so intimate, they became as one.

Morning found them unashamed, his royal robes covering their naked bodies as the wings of a swan protecting her young. He was lost in his rapture for he had found her. Her gentle words poured over his spirit and cooled the angry embers within him. She mellowed and yet invigorated until his heart was full of her.

"You are far more noble than me," he said repeatedly.

"I am neither noble nor plain. I am yours, Kareem, and yet I belong to nature as does every flower in the sand."

"I have found in you a wisdom that leads me to everlasting joy."

"You have found only me, Kareem. It is you who must discover joy, that which lives within you, and now, please come to me once more for I desire the pleasure of your body close to mine."

Kareem wooed her in the ways of a prince until her smooth, young body fell limp beneath him.

After a fortnight, Jama sent a messenger to find them.

"You must return at once, your highness," the boy stammered. "Your father is dying."

The royal funeral was splendid.

"My father would have loved all this," Kareem confided to Sara with a tinge of shame.

"Perhaps he found God in the end," Sara said simply. "We do not know these

"Do you think he did?"

"Yes, I think so."

"Sara, after all he did to you- -to us, how can you feel this way?"

"I just do, that's all, Kareem. It is a comfort to me and I do believe it."

Kareem reigned with Sara for one year before she revealed the message to him.

"I have seen goodness, Kareem. I have been taken into the light."

"Sara."

"I have conceived of a son who will bring the word to all corners of the earth."

"God."

And the word was made flesh and dwelt amongst them for one million years. And the earth was glorified and yet death came slowly, though the seed remained frozen until the next warming.

CHAPTER TWO
AND DARKNESS DESCENDED
OVER THE EARTH

The sky light above Aavaar had vanished with nightfall. He stared up into its black emptiness and wondered how long he had been alone.

A few dim lights flickered impotently on the instrument panel in front of him, but the scanner was empty. He stretched forth his long limbs and yawned languidly. Suddenly he was cold and tired.

He thought of home. It would be the twilight hour now. He allowed his old memories to envelop him warmly, remembering the golden liquid that splashed over rocks sending rose and helio mist high up into the atmosphere.

"One more dawn," he whispered as though praying. "There are white, hot embers deep within my being that are wild with yearning to be stirred up again. I must not let them die too soon."

His thoughts took him back to the day of his transfiguration. It was hot that day. He tried to find a place in the shade, but there was no shade.

His parents would have reached the city by now, having found comfort within the confines of a cool, damp building somewhere. He wondered if they had missed him yet. He had lingered too long to watch a nesting bird, and the caravan had left him behind.

Brown sand stretched across the desert in front of him and on both sides. The air was motionless, allowing the heat to pour over him until it became unbearable and his thirst was great. No creature stirred. He hated himself for dallying. He drew his stole up over his face and tried to keep going onward, but the light about him became so intense he was paralyzed by it. At once, he was drawn up into a presence that he was never able to define.

He awakened near the entrance of a building where his mother stood weeping. They did not believe Aavaar.

"He is simple," Aavaar's mother said, "a foolish juvenile. We must not pay attention to his stories for fear of encouraging him."

The people accused him of babbling foolish absurdities and, to some extent, the youth was shunned. "The light does not come to the likes of him," they said.

When Aavaar began to conduct simple experiments that had miraculous results, he was called before the Council of Scientific Scholars. He poured forth knowledge unto them that had no limits. He became revered in the community and, by the age of twenty-nine, was known throughout the galaxy as a Deolite, or one who had spoken with (God) the light.

His lessons to them were transcribed in granite, and research in every field of scientific development was initiated because of them.

At the age of thirty-three, a band of jealous scholars of superior heritage set out to destroy him. Once again, he was taken up by the light.

When he returned, the real days of his glory began.

. . . .

A dull, humming sound drew him back into the present.

He drew his fingers over a blank spot on the panel, and a huge metal door opened automatically. A young scientist slipped in and showed Aavaar her identification. Without speaking, she sat down at her station and snapped a flask of hot liquid into place as she did so.

"Have you not eaten?" Aavaar asked.

"No, sir," she replied without looking at him.

"How long have you been outside?" he asked. Her silence was answer enough.

"I see," Aavaar said. "I shall not keep you waiting the next time."

She started to speak, but Aavaar raised his hand to silence her and left.

"Have you eaten today?" Aavaar asked when she returned for her shift the next day.

"Yes, sir," she responded indifferently. She was very beautiful, this one.

"Tell me your name," Aavaar said. He knew it very well.

"I am Feleecia," she said, and slipped professionally into her seat before the scanner.

"What do you think of the new Plasma Scope?"

"It's . . . magnificent," she groped for the word.

"An inanimate scientific genius, Moross calls it. He thinks it is living, I believe."

"Moross is a wise and benevolent prime minister."

"Do you know him?"

"Yes, he is a friend of my father's."

"Ah."

"I am Ettoiville," she said.

"You have a right to your pride."

"Thank you."

A buzzing sound announced the entrance of another young scientist.

"Oh! Forgive me," she looked startled to see Aavaar still there.

"Feleecia, they need you at the Paulo Station. I am to replace you," she said.

"The Paulo Station; that is Ragaar's post," Aavaar thought. Even Aavaar knew what that meant. He was disappointed.

"You many both leave," he said quietly. "I will stay. I wish to work alone tonight".

Navrid came up with some hot tea a little later. She knew that he would be needing her. Navrid had been with Aavaar for many years. She was not of his kind, and so they could not unite. Therefore, their love was deep. She left quietly as she had come, which was her way.

Feleecia returned unexpectedly and entered without requesting permission. Aavaar was excited by her presence.

"Are you all right, Feleecia," Aavaar asked.

"You are a Deolite, Aavaar. You have been in the presence of God. I could not know that," Feleecia whispered. "Forgive me."

"The light is with us this very moment, Feleecia. There is nothing to forgive."

"I'll stay now," Feleecia said.

"That is good for I am tired."

Feleecia began spending much time with Aavaar, and the crew mumbled among themselves.

"Ragaar is no more than a pot of wet porridge to her now," one of them said.

36

"No matter, the pot bubbles," another retorted.

It was no secret that Ragaar considered the old one a false prophet, if indeed the light existed at all.

"I have prayed to be taken up since I was a little child," Feleecia confided one evening to Aavaar.

"It does not happen that way, Feleecia."

"But, Aavaar, I desire it so. It is all I have lived for since childhood when I learned of the revelations."

"It is with you now; it is ever present."

"No, no it isn't, not in the same way. Aavaar, I want to be taken up as you were and filled with knowledge to pass on to my people."

"To be great and powerful and revered as very nearly a deity as I once was?"

"No! I desire the knowledge, Aavaar. My soul yearns for it. I crave answers, Aavaar."

"You mustn't crave anything, Feleecia. The light is here. I know that and yet I feel no different now than I did as a youth before it came to me. I am the same."

"That is impossible."

"When I first laid eyes upon you, I desired to be young again. Is that God-like, Feleecia?"

"I can't believe you."

"It is true. The light gave me knowledge which has reached every star in the galaxy. It asked me to give love also, and in that I have failed, failed myself, failed my people, failed 'the light'."

"Love?"

"Slaves need love to exist, to survive. It is not for . . ."

"An Ettoiville."

"Aavaar, love is for slaves!"

"Are they not blessed if this is true?"

Feleecia left him alone and once more Navrid came to him. "It cannot be taught, it must come," she comforted.

For the next few days, Feleecia avoided Aavaar, and he was lonely.

"I am old," he said to Navrid, "and yet I do not believe it. I yearn for the love of a young one who finds disgust in the very mention of the word."

"You must show them how."

"To love?"

"Yes."

"Your kind knows love from the beginning of life."

"That is so, but there are only nine of us left. I tell you, it cannot be taught, Aavaar. It must be lived. Your people had it once in the beginning. Their cruelty destroyed it. It was destroyed in the mothers first. When women become loveless, their children die in the starvation of sadness. One must first be loved that later he may give love."

"My mother wept over me once."

"She was unusual," Navrid said softly and then left him alone.

"Will it come to me Aavaar?" Feleecia pleaded the next day.

"It comes to everyone."

"You have a gift. Use it, Feleecia. Many things are more important than scientific discovery. Love is one of them."

"Love?"

"It is powerful."

"Did the light give you that?"

"Yes, before that I understood nothing."

"I believe you, Aavaar."

"I love you, Feleecia."

She was radiant during those days with Aavaar. They cherished their hours together, and Feleecia began to change. Aavaar's tales of his glorification never bored her.

"Continue to study, for the book is not mine, but comes from the light."

Only days later, Feleecia was summoned home. No reason was given. The order came from Moross.

When the shuttle departed that day, two souls were depleted. Aavaar slipped into deep melancholia. Once again, Navrid came to comfort him.

Feleecia's replacement was called Marga. Aavaar offered his welcome to her upon her arrival in his laboratory.

She is cool, this one, Aavaar thought, very young to be so esteemed by her colleagues. He still lives in the past, the young one decided. Aavaar started to leave when an alarm alerted the two of them.

"Hello, what is this?" the young scientist became excited.

At first, the audio was bad. A burst of crackling sounds was preceded by a dull, unusual hum. Aavaar gave Marga a signal to be silent and neither moved. A definite image began to fade in and out of the visual portion of the scanner. It began to sparkle at first, and then showed up as a black sphere with a bluish aura.

For hours, the old and young scientists remained together watching. When exhaustion defeated Aavaar, the young one remained alone at the station for long hours on into the night.

In the weeks that followed, Aavaar became a prisoner of his fascination. Marga lost interest after a few days when nothing concrete could be documented. "My superiors want data," she had confronted Aavaar.

"She wants glory," Aavaar surmised.

For the most part, the rest of the crew showed no interest in the sphere either; moreover, they considered Aavaar's use of the equipment a waste of precious instruments and time. It was such a small planet, one of only millions in the galaxy. They could not understand his enthusiasm.

"We need to do more important plasma studies," they murmured among themselves, "not waste time on stars without life."

One day without notice, Aavaar bolted into the space control room and yelled out an order to the startled navigator.

"I need the ancient trackings of Ufforis."

"Sir?"

"Get them immediately!"

He bolted back to the scanner.

"He is getting daft," the navigator mumbled. "He could have beamed me from his station."

Aavaar called for Marga. "Can you explain this?" He was wild with excitement!

"Nothing has changed," she said with a shrug of boredom.

"What do you see now?" he maneuvered the scanner.

"A weak sun." She was still not impressed.

"Look further," Aavaar pointed at the corner of the screen. "It is a star with nine planets circling it, each with a different surface."

Without enthusiasm she said, "And this means?"

"That one is Ufforis, paradise, earth."

"That? Paradise?"

"I am sure of it."

For days, Aavaar poured over the ancient reports and mappings. One day when he had very nearly given up hope, his joy returned. He found the ancient rings of Zercon. The very rings that showed up daily as the earth rotated on the screen before him. The Zercons had landed on earth a million years past and left records to be kept in the library of space long after their own planet had disintegrated.

The Zercons had landed in paradise.

Aavaar was sure he had rediscovered Paradise, the holiest place in the universe where the benevolent guidance of God and nature swelled to Euphoria, where souls would be reborn again to life everlasting.

Aavaar devoured the ancient book as he absorbed and reabsorbed its content.

The vision was clear. A sky of clearest blue, an atmosphere so clean that to take it to oneself and breathe it inward was to experience an emotion called happiness, or love of being. To gaze from the ship, below to its surface, was the first experience to excite the ancient ones, for there were magnificent waters of blue in all shades, from pale to darkest indigo, and mountains of rock in every color, and the land itself was green and copper or brown with trees and flowers of every variety. Nowhere else in the universe could they find such beauty.

Aavaar drew up into his mind every description of the place by the ancients and could dwell upon nothing else. The old being became fascinated beyond his wildest dream, and the vision of the planet as seen by the ancients swelled within his mind and filled his imagination to the point that he could very nearly touch the flowers and feel the water that rippled in the streams that they described. The vision was in his mind only, moreover, the atmosphere was not at all as it had been described. Its sun was weak, and the planet was shrouded in semi-darkness.

The crew continued to grumble among themselves. They could not afford to satisfy the whims of an arrogant, old Deolite who wanted only to glorify himself once again by the discovery of heaven.

They were very near mutiny when the order came to land.

Only Navrid would agree to leave the vessel, and had it not been for the magnificent space attire they wore, they would have both frozen immediately after touching earth's surface, for there was no sign of life- -not one living particle.

The pull of gravity was strong, and the surface was so slippery that the pair could have fallen down forcefully, dashing themselves against sharp, jutting masses of frozen hydrogen and oxygen, had they not been aptly suited up.

Aavaar decided to give up his dream. It was Navrid who changed all that by asking, "Why would the ancient ones lie? This is Ufforis. I am certain of it."

For Aavaar, those words were too challenging to dismiss.

"Could the ancient ones have been influenced by the natural hallucinogen upon their decent?" he wondered out loud.

"No, I don't think so. It would have been later recorded," Navrid said.

"What should I do, old friend of mine?" Aavaar asked.

"I would like to stay and explore," she said. "Your dream is mine, also."

For two years, the two old scientists roamed over the ice, drilling and searching as they made their way over six thousand miles of the earth's surface. At times, the silence was eerie and the stillness terrifying. Aavaar felt as though a great and angry God watched quietly from the distance. They found nothing but ice and darkness.

Sometimes, suddenly out of the stillness, a hideous blizzard would blow up, and even Navrid made fun of the ancient ones and their description of Paradise.

At last, one day when a terrible storm was crossing the earth's surface, Aavaar gave up the search and begged his crew to land and pick them up. Just after ascension, as he was staring downward at the circles made by the rays of their craft, the most thunderous, rumbling sounds ever heard in the universe erupted as the great masses of frozen water began shifting.

Somehow this interaction with the liquid deep below caused a movement on earth unparalleled in time.

Their scanners now picked up mountains of rock beneath the ice. The shifting continued, making grooves in the great subterranean rocks, sometimes diminishing them in size as it hurled matter of enormous proportion downward for hundreds of miles. For days, the ice roared downward, breaking and crumbling mountains in its thunderous outburst. The ship's crew recorded the happenings for the first time with fascination, for they believed the planet was indeed disintegrating.

When it was over, Navrid said softly one evening, "There was once life in abundance. I am certain of it."

"Has it gone forever, my friend?" the old one smiled.

"It has gone for now," she replied, "and our young crew wishes to study the plasma of which outer space is made. It is just."

Old Aavaar was relieved of his duties upon his return to the planet, and when he left, no one, save Navrid, believed him to be a Deolite. The light did not return while he lived, but the galaxy came alive with rumors.

WOMAN
OF
THE SECOND WARMING

In the beginning, when the first daughter cell separates, all human life is female. In this sense, we have the natural superiority of womankind. The ultimate and most powerful necessity of male, and his importance in the galaxy, can be understood as we discover the complex cascade that determines maleness.

Every human embryo begins as female, but more than half become male during the natural process. At this point there is no superiority, but only mutual need to continue in the galaxy. In this sense neutrality is superior as it directs the unification of male and female into one flesh.

The greatest, as well as the most fragile, must harmonize in order to survive, for only in blending with the natural elements, too vast for comprehension, can we be sustained in life, . . . love, . . . and in the hereafter.

CHAPTER THREE
THE WARMING

Ten thousand years after the departure of Aavaar, the warming of earth began. A droplet of water appeared and began to trickle downward, meeting other forming drops on its way. Narrow streams formed and gained inertia as they flowed downward.

In time, after thousands of years, great swells of rushing, bubbling white and blue magnificence cleansed all of the earth and brought new life to the planet.

Mountains rose above the rushing waters, and peaks of purple granite thrust their majestic summits out into the sunlight.

Earth's moon drew on the waters and the rivers rushed downward to form seas full of minerals swept from the rocks. Great oceans were formed that cracked and separated the planet's surface, allowing portions to break off and float away.

As the moon kept pulling, its strength became enormous. The sun grew stronger too, and darkness was lifted forever.

The trees and plants that sprang up gave off pure oxygen and took in carbon dioxide, so that the atmosphere was clean and perfect.

Many species came to dwell upon the earth, but millions of years passed before came the link to humanae.

SHE WAS WOMAN

She came out of the Southern Hemisphere and was the shade of charred cinder. She was perfect. She had a round head, capped in soft down the color of black lamb's wool. Her eyes were magnificent. Her nostrils flared, and her lips were full. She was youth.

She had no memory of her coming and was quite alone among the animals. Though they gave her comfort, she slept apart from them, but could communicate with every species.

Her senses were keen. She understood the rumblings of the forest and skies.

She learned when to take shelter, but most of all, she learned how to survive, for she was alone.

She sensed the changing of seasons, but did not know how many she had lived.

During autumn, her body began to change. Two separate, soft bulges swelled beneath her shoulders. At the tip of each was a protrusion that at times became quite erect and hurt her. She became encumbered by the size of her swelling body and could no longer bend over easily.

One evening, a sensation that was not pleasant shrunk her belly and forced its pain down below it. Another twinge caused her to wince and she wanted to sit down, but that position wan no longer comfortable. For some time, she had been feeling unusual, poking sensations that pressed and pressed against her belly from inside of it, but this was different, and for the first time in her life on earth, she began to cry. The strange blows from within converged into one very strong, contracting pain.

She squatted down and supported herself by clutching a thick, low-hanging vine. The sensations came more frequently and grew stronger. She began to grunt and moan, but could not move. A slush of warm water gushed between her legs. She grasped the vine with all her might and pushed down as hard as she could. It was in this way that the first man was born.

She slipped backwards into the grass. He wailed loudly. She glance downward. It looked like no animal she had ever seen.

She felt her belly. It was hollow and soft. A lump that was hard and round bobbled under her hand. She felt a plop that originated within her slurp between her legs. It was slimy, as was the newborn and was, in fact, attached to it by a cord that was white and slimy also, and seemed to have something beating inside of it. She grasped it between her fingers and it stopped pulsating.

She had seen only one animal birth, that of a claw-footed prowler. That animal's mother had chewed at the cord of her offspring and then eaten the soft, reddish blob that had come out of her.

The infant was now squealing loudly. She chewed at the cord and licked the surface of the part she had severed. The infant stopped its wailing and fell asleep.

They slept and awakened together. She took him with her to the water, for they were hot. She slipped into the liquid coolness and bathed the child. In the clear water, she could see her limbs below her. A gush of red came up from between her legs, but quickly dispersed and the water cleared once again. She released the baby into the water, and it began to move its limbs. She watched as it pulled and kicked the water. She lifted it up to take the air and it squealed mightily. She held it high and laughed.

She took it to the land and placed it on her breast where it nestled comfortably. A bluish-white liquid spilled out of her nipples and ran down near its mouth. While still asleep, he moved his tongue and lips, and she laughed once again as he tasted it. She put his mouth about her nipple and he suckled heartily.

48

From that time on, they clung to each other as though he was still a part of her body.

He began to grow and his form changed. His black eyes stared up into her own whenever she suckled him, and she laughed aloud when, afterwards, he imitated her grimaces.

Love filled her heart with great joy, and she could think of nothing else, save her tiny companion.

One day, she offered him a berry. He swished it around in his mouth and then rolled it out with his tongue. She took a larger, firmer fruit and chewed it herself until it was mushy, and then spooned it into his mouth with her fingers. When she stopped, he squealed for more. Soon he had eaten the whole fruit. Each day thereafter, she gave him more and gradually increased the variety. By now he was crawling and clinging to rocks and ledges to pull himself up. He grew two teeth. They came in at the bottom in the middle of his gums. He walked soon after and then ran. His body began to take on a shape nearly like her own, and pretty soon he no longer desired the milk of her breasts, but pushed his head away or rolled it from side to side when it was offered. Her breasts dried up and went back to their original firmness, nearly flat upon her chest muscle.

To her delight, he began to imitate all the animal and bird sounds.

One day, he spoke out a word of his own, "Daa." She laughed. "Daa, Daa, Daa," she sang out and he laughed, too, and repeated the word.

She called him Daa, and then one day he made another sound, "Naanam." "Naa Nam," she repeated and, thenceforth, she called herself Naa-nam.

Her offspring was different from her chiefly in one way- -the protrusion below between his legs.

As the long days passed and he grew to be taller than she herself, they became equal as children growing up together. They used some sign language to communicate, but mostly that was only a game of childhood. Their telepathic communication was so keen that even when they were separated by some distance, they could communicate easily. If, for example, Daa had strayed down the riverbank too far and Naa-nam saw a storm brewing in the East, she need only to think the word Daa to break into his mind, and he could see the storm clouds as easily as she herself standing directly beneath them. As time went by, they sent telepathic messages back and forth at will. She thinking the word Daa to break in and he the word Naa-nam, his very own first original words.

They flashed images back and forth to one another that were as clear as if they were present on the spot where it was taking place. But when they were together, they did not disturb the thoughts of one another except to communicate. This they did with love, for they were a gentle couple, and the universe of their brains began to thrive and increase naturally because of this love.

The memory of Daa's birth became so pushed back in Naa-nam's mind that eventually when Daa pondered the question, "How did we come to be here?" she answered with honesty, "I don't know."

They grew strong, he by now was much taller. She admired him, as well as loved him. He began to measure distance with paces or footprints on the sand. He found a pole to measure height. He watched the sun's rising and setting and told her when night would fall.

From the earliest days of what really was childhood for both of them, they had played and rolled about on the sand or splashed together in the river. They were used to their bodies touching, and they loved the feel of each other as they slept in the grass or rolled over a soft dune. But they never explored below and had no desire to do so. They watched the animals mate with fascination and sometimes give birth as well. But they felt no stirring, as yet.

Then one day, as they rolled and played by the river, something different happened. Naa-nam felt the blunt hardness of something between her legs pressing on her inner thigh. Daa looked down at himself and was frightened. Naa-nam put the vision of two beautiful mating swans into his mind. She looked at him for a long time and his part continued to remain erect. She smiled at him and went forth into the water to wade until she was nearly ankle deep. It was then that she did a most unusual thing. She dropped first onto her knees and then pressed her hands before her out into the sand in the shallow water. She then stretched her bottom up towards him as high as she could. He came to her and swept his arms around her waist and then gently up to her breasts as the wings of the mating swan and pressed himself forth into her.

Naa-nam dipped her face in and out of the clear, lovely water and the throbbing within her grew stronger and stronger, until she could bear it no longer, and she cried out with the joy of it. He, too, sobbed out loudly, for he could not stop now had he wanted to. When it was over, they sat staring wide-eyed and bewildered. "What happened?" Daa asked, and then he smiled at her. "I don't know," she said, for she was puzzled also. Then she reached out for him and pulled his head down upon her breast. They sat quietly for a long time looking out over the water and then Daa took her hand and led her back inland. "Look," he said, "the sun is beginning to set. It will soon be nightfall." She marvelled at his wisdom and was in awe of his manhood.

Thereafter, each springtime, Naa-nam gave birth to a child until it had happened nine times. At first, they were all replicas of Daa, born with large organs between their legs. Each was taken to the water. The bath became man's first ritual and took on a sacredness, if such a word can be used to describe those prehistoric times.

Finally, after ten births, to the delight of the couple, a female was born, and after that there followed four more.

When her children grew strong and the first ones began mating, she smiled upon them and remembered with love her own, very first experience with Daa, and while her children were not monogamous by any means, she and Daa remained so, for they were full of love for each other. No jealousy or hatred prevailed yet upon the earth. Life in the truest sense was simple, for food was plentiful and needed only to be gathered. For the most part, the elements in that millennium were kind and the temperature continued to rise and warm the earth.

Daa loved his children, their children, and their children's children. The males liked to gather around him, for he taught them many things.

The females stayed near the cave with Naa-nam. They developed a complicated, sign language and even made up new sounds to describe things. The females nursed their offspring and guarded the small children. The males were the providers, and with each generation, they strayed farther and farther from the settlement. None were ever lost, and telepathic communication remained their chief means of correspondence.

Soon, there were many hundreds of children and they began breaking off into bands or segments while still remaining one large family.

For several generations, there was a shortage of females, and so the males would share them kindly with each other and protect and provide for them, as well as their offspring. No one knew who belonged to whom. Even the mothers exchanged babies to feed.

A problem arose at one time when one of the males wanted to bear a child. He could not understand why he should not have this privilege. He usually stayed around the settlement with the females. He learned their sign language well and cared for the babies as did the adolescent girls. He was convinced that he could bear a child if only one of his brothers or cousins would copulate with him as they did with his sisters. The other males were not interested. The boy became a favorite of his grandmother, not that all of her children weren't special in their own way. She smiled upon him and loved him very much as did the other girls, and though his brothers loved him, too, they did not understand why he would want to stay behind and miss all the wonders and new discovery that they enjoyed with Daa.

In his segment, there happened to be more males than females. After much pleading with his cousins, both telepathically and through signs, he persuaded one of the males to perform for him in the way they had all witnessed since babyhood, that his elders and peers did, for everyone usually gathered around to witness a mating unless it happened quite unexpectedly out away from the settlement. Usually one mating inspired many more and this delighted the now elders of the clan.

This time, the mating inspired no one, and the boy who performed it did not like it. Still, Aab, the one who wanted to bear a child, believed that come springtime he would have a baby of his own.

It didn't happen and he was sad, very sad. Naa-nam called him to her side.

"Look to the animals," she said in the sign language that he had so deftly learned. "Those like you cannot give birth. Only we, the women, can do that, but without you, the males, we cannot survive. You protect us, you provide for us better than the animals do for their own kind. You are special. You are man. Without you we are nothing. Without us you are nothing, for only you can give us children and bring pleasure to our souls. I believe we have an organ within us where the child grows. You have not such a room in your body, for you are man. You must be content with that."

After that, the boy remained near the cave, but he did not mate with the females. He cared for the children, and one day, many years later, a male child came to him and said, "I want to bear a child. will you copulate with me?" And they did, and they loved each other, but no child was ever born. Still they cherished each other and the family said, "It is their way."

Naa-nam closed her eyes and did not awaken after the birth of her last child which came very late in her life. The child was robust and taken to the breast of another woman. Daa took his mate to the little sea and swam very far out with her to where it was black and its depth unknown. As the sun disappeared over the horizon, so did the couple go with it.

Aab tried desperately hard to communicate with them, first Daa and then Naa-nam to no avail. He stopped all communications with the others, even the one he loved, and when the boy left him to mate with his sister, Aab felt within him great sadness. He swam out to the blackness of the little sea and was lost. No one was troubled, for he had left no seed upon the earth and his life gave nothing to the world.

For thousands of years, the descendants of Naa-nam roamed the earth, happily gathering food and reproducing in abundance, and the warming continued. They wandered out in every direction.

The earth divided itself once again, and part of it floated away, separating the land by great oceans.

As friendly tribes continued to form, the male elders became the Daa's, or protectors.

THE TRIBE OF KIR

The tribe of Kir was the first to journey Northward where they found lakes and rivers with fish in abundance. With each century, the migration Northward continued.

It was Da-Kir who awakened with a great chill one morning in winter and discovered the phenomenon of snow.

They survived that winter by huddling together with animals in small caves.

These people had long fingers and were deft at toolmaking. They chipped at flint stone and made spear tips. They had already learned to fashion a harpoon by fastening a sharply honed stone to the tip of a pole, and now they learned how to make and keep fires kindling.

That winter of the first snow, they used the fur of dead animals to protect themselves from the winter's cold.

The skin of their offspring lightened with succeeding generations, and the first child born with yellow fuzz atop its head was thought to be a freak. Soon there were many of his coloring. They inter-married freely and produced a human colourant variation that was superb.

It was by accident that the first animal was killed by man. Kir, the father of the ancient tribe, was troubled by the animal's killing of each other. His great-grandfather had witnessed the first such incident. It had grown cold and the vegetation was sparse that year. For the most part, the animals could not fish as man did. One day, a large, fierce cat leapt from above and fell down upon a cow, killing her almost instantly and ravaging her flesh while devouring her. Kir tried to forget the incident, but as the years passed, he was grieved to see more and more animal killings. He noted that those who ate the flesh of other animals bore offspring even more vicious than their predecessors. Moreover, he loved the little animals who usually were their victims. In time, only the grazing animals remained docile while, with each generation, the meat-eaters grew larger and fiercer.

"One day, they will attack man," he warned his great-grandson, Slo. "I warn you, the day will come when man will be no more safe than the gentle doe." The claw-footed animals were the most dangerous and cunning. Those who grazed remained quiet and nurturing towards their young. Meat-eaters roamed off alone to kill.

Slo loved to fish, as well as gather. As did his forbearer, he also loved the small animals, many of which scurried right up to his ankles. The ponds were overflowing with fish and mussels. There was no hunger as yet. The people settled near the lakes where food was abundant even in the colder months. Still the fierce animals hunted.

It was near the lake where the slaughter occurred. A large cat appeared and suddenly, without warning, lunged out and snapped up a plump, brown pup that had been playfully following Slo. To save him, Slo jabbed the cat with his harpoon. The tip of his flint-tipped harpoon caught the animal directly in his left eye. It lunged forward, but then fell convulsing on the ground before him. Slo knew that if the animal got up, he would kill him. The great cat moaned and rolled to one side. Slo knew he must finish it now. He drew up his harpoon and speared the animal through the heart. Its' blood spurted out and covered his hands and face. The pup ran off. Slo, still trembling, walked to the water's edge and began to bathe the blood from his person. It was then that a strange and dreadful feeling overtook his very soul. The feeling was excitement.

Slo taught his people to fashion even better spears with larger, flint-head stones to protect themselves from the animals.

"Man must control the beasts," he told them, remembering the words of his grandfather. "They are wild. They will kill us all otherwise."

Hundreds of years passed before the people killed animals, not just to protect themselves, but for their flesh and hides.

It happened gradually- -first in one tribe and then another. At first, most of the women objected. "Because the animals eat flesh, does that mean we should, also?" One wise, old grandmother said, "We are not beasts. See how violent the meat-eaters are? We will become as animals. Why, soon, we will be killing each other." The others laughed at that thought. "Man will never kill man, old one," they said. But she scoffed and said, "We have honey and fruit in abundance and fish, too. Look into the waters. They come right to the surface for our taking. We must not eat the flesh of animals or we will become as animals."

Still, the excitement persisted among the men and the kill became an event that aroused within their souls an exhilaration that rivaled no other. When they sat around the fire in the evenings, the conversation was of nothing else. They boasted of their cunning in tracking and laughed proudly about the bravery of one or the other. They danced about the fire imitating the exact movements of the wild beasts, and the one who did the best imitation was cheered and urged on.

It was only a matter of time before the meat was brought back to the fire and someone discovered how delicious was a portion that had fallen upon the embers.

Soon, the women and children participated in the feast, and animal hides were used as clothing. When one of the men dressed himself in animal fur taken from a great cat, an old woman grumbled, "Now you see, he even looks like the animal."

The people had become not only fishermen and gatherers, but hunters as well. Many became wanderers who followed their prey.

Other tribes stayed in one location. These were the cave dwellers who cherished permanent settlements. They lived by the ponds and large lakes and were fulfilled. They gathered and fished and relaxed, working no more than eighty hours in a given month. They were a happy people and killed animals only out of necessity.

These peoples tried to build cave-like structures near the water, and the only real toil they ever knew was in moving great boulders to build the first, man-made, permanent residences on earth. This took place in Europe and East Asia long before the pyramids of Egypt were thought of, and these curious stone monuments exist even today from Northern Scotland and Ireland across Great Britain and even into Portugal.

The hunters preferred temporary dwellings which they made of great animal antlers and horns that formed the rounded framework. The frame was covered by animal skins which they unfastened and carried with them when they left in search of food. It was then used over again for the next shelter. Sometimes the hunters amassed the bones of nearly a thousand animals in one settlement. Their life was harder now, and the excitement of the kill even stronger.

Nighttime rituals following the hunt became almost as pleasant as the kill itself, the ritualistic dance depicting the life story of the fallen animal became almost artistic. And when the dancer made his final fall to the ground in the simulation of death, the others fell silent in reverence before rising to cheer and participate in the exhilaration.

Soon chanting and humming became a part of the scene. Then came the beating of drum-like instruments made from stretching skins over hollow logs.

In time, whistles were made from the hollow tips of antlers and then pipes of bamboo. Thus, music and dance came to the earth.

This was not the only artistic endeavor during this millennium. In the caves, the first paintings of man began to appear. Most were of animals quite often pregnant. Paints and colors were ingeniously created that would last for thousands of years. Sculpture also was initiated, sometimes chiseled from granite or marble stone. Men and women alike participated in this pastime. Men chiseled beautiful heads of young girls with swollen bellies. They had become good at toolmaking, as well as tool using. It was the art era, the beginning of it all.

The flesh-eaters grew bigger and much stronger. So did they become more fierce, and alas, soon the excitement of the animal kill was not enough. They became a vile and raucous group. Sometimes the men returned only to mate and no longer provided for the women and children, but just rather prowled alone.

Jealousy erupted when one such man returned and stole a woman away from her dwelling and raped her repeatedly. Two of her other mates killed the man later, and his body was tossed over a cliff for the scavengers.

It had all started as the old woman predicted. There was a millennium of terrible violence on the earth.

Men became superstitious. They came to see the moon and sun as gods, and it was not long before animals were sacrificed to them. Stone figures were carved and worshipped, also, while they danced and chanted in the moonlight. During these times, the first carving of an image that was half man and half animal appeared on earth which was predictable, for that is what man was fast becoming. It was not long before humans, as well as animals, were sacrificed to the evil gods that had been created.

Something most dramatic occurred during this era, however. The most gentle people began to find each other and pair off. They slipped away and formed separate families apart from the violence of the other society. When a mate was needed for a son or a daughter, they would search for another family such as their own.

By now, the gift of telepathy had vanished from earth, but sign language had become such an art that they were able to communicate easily.

The mothers decided whether or not the union would be good. If it was decided upon, the young couple was permitted to go off alone for seven days. The young man was encouraged to fondle and explore the maiden's body to discover her opening. Only if she loved and accepted him must their bodies unite.

In this way, the men learned to become gentle lovers and very few maidens rejected this ancient courtship, and they, too, became gentle lovers in return. Thus was the beginning of monogamy.

The first actual marriage ceremony came about in this way; when a father gave of his child to be united with another, the two being joined stood and faced one another with their fathers at their sides. Each father placed his hand on the head of his child. When the couple joined hands, the fathers swiftly removed their hands and motioned the air as though assisting a young bird to fly away. Remember, the people were fluent in sign language.

One day at the union of a maiden called Sheanna and a youth named Daavid, an extraordinary thing happened just as the fathers released the couple with their gesture. All of the members simultaneously reached out and took the hand of the person standing next to him until the couple was surrounded by a ring of loving relatives. Someone began to hum and the circle began to move in a dance. Thereafter, at each union, a simple ceremony took place.

The first to offer her husband a dowry was a girl called Zievra who was a skilled sculptor. She carved out of stone the image of a beautiful fish. Her husband, in turn, went to the pond and caught twelve, plump, white fish. That evening, the fish were baked by the fire and shared with all those present. This, too, became a custom until, in time, weddings became synonymous with feast. It also enforced the notion of man or husband as provider.

During this millennium, another wonderful thing happened. The hybridization of wheat began somewhere in what is now Iraq, or Iran.

Small seeds fattened on the swaying grasses, were borne by the wind to other parts of the earth.

When Zievra discovered it for the first time in her part of the world, she showed Aaman, her husband.

"See how the little sprouts come up near the grass where the seedlings have fallen," she said to him. "They are fat, these seedlings up top." She plucked off a stem and laid it on a flat stone to examine it more closely. She dropped the small boulder she had been holding. It smashed down upon the wheat and powdered it. Zievra wet her finger and tasted the powder. She liked it.

At the same time, everywhere people were discovering wheat flour and it was not long before water and fat were added to the mixture to make cakes. Soon after that, baking them on hot stones over the fire was initiated. Zievra herself added honey, smearing it over the tops of her cakes. "They are delicious," her husband said smiling proudly down upon his wife. "What will you call them?"

"Manna," she responded. "I will call them manna."

Thus, the grinding of grain was begun and the bread of life discovered.

As time went on, the gentle families were driven far and wide by the vicious hunters. Wherever they went, they built the huge stone monuments. They became a symbol of peace and shelter, and wherever they were found, the land was considered scared. Zievra herself had probably been one of the very first farmers.

Noting that new grass sprang up wherever a seedling dropped, she gathered a handful of seeds and sprinkled them near the dwelling. A soft wind blew them all away, or so she thought, and so she forgot about her experiment for several days until she saw the sprouts pushing their way up through the soft soil all in a row, the very way she had placed them. She became ecstatic. The kindly breeze had only just covered them with the nourishing, black sand. By the next season, she had planted a whole field of wheat for her cakes. The people were in awe of her intelligence and began to treat her very nearly as a goddess.

Soon the men and women were gathering and planting wheat, and that year the first crop was bountiful.

Families began to mark off territories with low stone walls and primitive ploughs, and by the end of that millennium, sheep and cattle were herded for their milk and wool. The wildest of the two species was the sheep. They were strong and athletic and did not take well to subjugation to man. And yet as time went on, they became the gentlest of all animals.

Women learned to sew up animal hides with the tough, long grasses. Then came the braiding of wool into clothing, and then decades later, they mastered the spinning of yarn.

Earth's peoples had divided into two groups- -the hunters and the farmers. Each group in its own way brought with it knowledge to be passed forward to future generations.

The wisdom of man brought within courage and a desire to explore. It was an intelligence that was different from women's. Man needed to discover new things and apply each discovery to searching for yet another.

Womankind needed to communicate to fill from within, to love and be loved. The dwelling was her prehistoric castle. The elements were his, and, so as woman looked out to the wondrous sky above her and the beauteous plants and flowers right there at her feet, and yearned to communicate love and feelings, so did the man look out to the wilderness and yearn to explore it. Such were the children of Zievra.

MARA

She was the gentle daughter of Zievra. She loved from her heart every person and thing. She talked to the creatures about her and would not destroy even the insect.

She looked up to the sky and could become absorbed in it. She was simple and beautiful. She needed little to survive, save love. She was woman.

She had only one brother, Ama, and she was full of him. She loved him, perhaps even more then her mother and father.

When they were very little, Ama showed her how to plant some wheat the way their mother had taught him. After that, she planted seedlings of every kind. It was really this little one who was to show the family that what her mother had done with the wheat could be done with many other species of plants.

Ama was proud of her. More and more, she began doing things to please him. Both children were gentle.

One evening, during a ceremony by the light of a silver slice of moon, a beautiful, young couple, barely more than children, were married. Mara joined hands with Ama around them as the families chanted their loving for the betrothed couple. Everyone was so happy. Even Zievra, the hostess, forgot her troubling feelings about her own two offspring.

Mara was so excited by the ritual that she felt a lovely dampness within her. Ama smiled and gently caressed the fingers that clutched his own. He smiled at her and forgot about the other couple. When the ritual was over, they slipped away.

Her body was brown and soft as silk. Her soul knew nothing but love. She was woman. She knew love, and she cherished his manhood.

At that moment, he came to her almost as a spirit. He opened her body and pressed his manhood gently within her. She caressed him with the warmth of her inner body and they united as one. They came together that night and found love forever.

They were brother and sister.

They were man and woman.

They were husband and wife.

It was good; during those times. It would take many more centuries before these unions were considered inappropriate, but it did happen gradually, more because of the simple attraction that occurs so often when one meets a stranger.

Mara and Ama had twenty-four sons and daughters, and all were sound in body and mind, but not one married a sibling, and the love of this gentle couple sprinkled the earth with flowers. Every son left his family to join the family of his wife or journey with her to discover new lands. They discovered much. They learned much. They planted and sowed; they gathered and fished; they painted and carved, and life on earth again was abundant, for it flourished and they knew not want. Evil did not exist in the hearts of these gentle people.

THE TWO GROUPS

As I have said, most of the earth's people were gathered into two groups--the hunters and the farmers.

For the most part, even the hunters were still a gentle people within their family segments. The violence and distrust came about when strangers were involved. Thus, they intermarried as a means of protection and out of fear of the other marauding tribes. When family produced too many sons, girls would be stolen from other camps.

Females were welcomed, for there seemed never to be enough and they were the mothers. Moreover, food was plentiful, and while the men hunted, the women gathered and fished.

The gentle farmers guarded their dwelling with spears and rock slings whenever the hunters came into their territory. They hid their daughters in caves- -each cave protected by three or four men who would have courageously given life if necessary.

While this group remained monogamous, polygamy was the norm among the hunters. Their feelings towards their women were different. Sensuality ran fevers through their bodies. Desire for the woman's body became the strongest of all drives within the men, and while they desired the women, they did not cherish them. Jealousy among the sexes was commonplace, and even beatings began to occur - - male of female and sometimes even of child.

It was the beginning of the subordination of womankind. Its misery spread into what is now the Mideast.

The gentle farmers also migrated. Sometimes the people were drawn too far North or South. It was then that they had to face the elements, and often food was scarce during the winters or very hot summers with conditions of drought.

Even though wonderful discoveries were being made in all parts of the world, such as the finding of metals in the ground, especially copper which was melted over fires and used for utensils and then for buildings, life was not so easy any more. Toil took the place of recreation for most humans. No more could they lounge by the lakes collecting berries or fishing. For the farmer, there was land to be tilled and sown, flocks to be herded, grain to be ground, and cattle and sheep to be fed.

Little girls, as early as age five, were taught to grind down the grain into flour, pounding it between rocks until, by the age of twenty, they were full of arthritic deformity and lived in great pain until death. The deformities showed up mostly in their spines, knees, and toes, for they knelt and rocked to grind the flour.

It became necessary for the women and children to do most of the work while the men guarded the settlements against wild animal attacks, or, what was worse, the marauding hunters.

Paganism and kings emerged at about the same time. Paganism, that is, in the form of not only sun and moon worship, but also of false Gods, such as sculptures of metal, gold, or granite, and many other talismans.

Savages set themselves up as witch doctors and kings, making all others subject to them and taking territories for themselves. War became inevitable and wickedness prevailed over much of the earth. Brutality turned its gaze upon the vulnerability of women, and it was not long before they were slaughtered as sacrifices to the gods. And in time, some of the descendants of the first mother on earth deteriorated into cruel, violent savages.

Still, there were those who cried out for a true God.

Mara was one such woman. She was a descendant of the first Mara, and she married a man called Ammaan.

During her last few years on earth, Mara took to slipping off alone to enjoy the beauty of the hillside. One day, she was drawn higher and higher until she was atop a peak so wonderful that the earth below gave the appearance itself of paradise.

It was there that the old woman rested until sunset. It was wondrous. The sky took on hues of orange and pink, blending with shades of blue and green and violet.

She watched the stars fall into a clear, endless, indigo sky and then nestled herself down to sleep upon a soft pillow of cord grass. The clean scent of the night's atmosphere brought tranquility into her soul, and her slumber was sweet.

Ammaan and her children came to regard her trips to the hillside as natural. They did not mind nor did they fear for her safety. Somehow, it was accepted that her wisdom exceeded their own.

When the heavens were clear, she would search the sky for hours and gradually become part of it.

When she came down from the mountain one day, she said, "I have felt the presence of God. There is only one, and there is no other. God is moral. God is goodness. God expects righteousness from the people, both man and woman. God will punish our transgressions. We are all equal in the heart of God."

Ammaan was astounded. His wife had indeed been transfigured. There was a radiance about her, and an aura of light surrounded her. Ammaan was afraid.

"Where is He?" he said trembling at the sight before him.

"God is not He," she said simply. "God is God."

Ammaan felt sorrow within his soul. "I do not understand, Mara," he said.

"Tomorrow you must come with me to the hilltop. Only then can you understand. You will feel the presence of God there, and you will know God as I do."

Old Ammaan experienced fatigue before they had even started the next day and begged Mara's understanding of his condition.

"No," Mara said firmly. "God desires your presence."

"Where does God abide, Mara?"

"God is everywhere. God is here within our hearts." She touched her breast.

"Then why must I, an old man, embark upon this perilous journey to the mountain-top? Mara, have you no heart for me anymore? Think of my age. I am weak now, and frail."

"You must come," Mara insisted. "It is the will of God."

Old Ammaan was near death when he reached the summit. Mara showed no concern, but merely smiled upon him in the way of a woman at peace.

The old man slowly came to his knees to rest. She comforted him then and fashioned a seat for him out of some firm shrubbery, covering it with soft grass and her own stole of lamb's wool. As she seated him there, she knelt beside him and wiped his tears with her hair.

"I am fatigued beyond my limits. I have no more endurance," he whispered.

"Sit quietly," she comforted him. "Say nothing, do not even think."

The old man obeyed his equally ancient wife and mentor.

The holy transfiguration came slowly. She felt it happening, first in his feeble hand as she kissed it. She stepped back and beheld the miracle from a distance.

He did not move. The milky glaze that had covered his eyes so worn out by age began to lift until his eyes glistened in childlike innocence. She witnessed him close then, while his lips moved, as though he was silently chanting. She understood and smiled, still in awe of the presence she knew was now here with both of them.

"God is everyone's God," she prayed, "and yet he has chosen us especially."

Ammaan became still as marble stone. An aura of violet emanated from within and formed a light to encircle his body. He opened his eyes and was radiant. He did not speak. They did not need to, for the light had filled their souls, and they understood and experienced great joy.

Ammaan fairly bolted down the mountainside. The vigor of his youth had been miraculously restored. He could not wait to tell the people and began to teach them immediately.

Mara died soon after the experience.

"Her soul was too full of joy to live," Ammaan told his children. "She has experienced heaven and has gone on ahead to prepare for our coming also."

Some of his children believed and were full of ecstasy as he was himself. This group went forth to bring the new religion eventually to all corners of the earth.

Still others felt that it should be a private religion kept to themselves within the family. This group chose to believe that there was no life after death, but rather that heaven or hell was right here upon earth.

Others believed that God was held within one's very soul, a private entity to be yours and yours alone.

Still, nearly all believed that God truly did exist, and even those who said they didn't could not be sure.

Ammaan died nearly forty years later after spreading the truth that would be continued forever.

The religion of the ancient ones, Ammaan and Mara, flourished and spread the world over. It came to pass that as their number grew, they tended to stay to themselves more and marry only members of their own religious body.

With the new religion, scholars emerged. At first these were only storytellers to spread the word of the only God concept.

As these stories were passed down from generation to generation, they would become more elaborate. When script was devised as a means to teach and relay the message of God, more and more writers of script began to emerge, each with his or her own story to tell. It was nearly all fiction produced by the imagination of the authors. Still, these scripts came to be considered sacred, and the authors were called teachers, or rabbi. As centuries passed, the collection of writings had become great. The script writing ceased and studying and translating the scriptures became the endeavor of the new rabbi. The scholars searched the ancient scripts for years trying to find answers to the problems of the people and to try to understand the mind and will of God, all to no avail.

In their search for meaningfulness, many men wasted a lifetime only to die without any answers at all. Most of the ancient authors described an angry, powerful, and vicious God, a punishing, merciless, even irrational one, who would murder children for laughing at a man who was bald. Perhaps, the author of that story had been a man without hair.

Nevertheless, more and more the scriptures came to be regarded as the sacred and true word of God. It was in this era that scripture became the law for the people.

Soon, this by now very large cult believed that they themselves were the chosen people of God, and that all people outside of their special family were heathens to be avoided and held in disdain as those of a very lowly caste.

Many years followed, and there was human bloodshed everywhere.

After one terrible defeat by the people of a place called Egypt, a large population of this religious cult who now called themselves Hebrew, which meant one from across the river, (the river being that which separated them from the heathens), was captured and taken away to be slaves.

From out of this captured population came an new teacher called Moses, and from out of Moses came the Torah, or the law which the people were to obey. Moses taught that God existed in the word and cared for all men. The children of Israel are no more to Him than the Ethiopians, and the law belongs to anyone who dares to claim it. Thus is the way of salvation for all mankind.

"The God of Moses is God" began to ring out across Egypt and beyond, and the scholars described a more merciful God than before.

It was during this period that many men, and women alike, began to experience the phenomenon of genetic memory, which caused great wonder among the scholars, for the natural ability to draw from memory cells had long since vanished. The gifted were both frightened and awed by their experiences. For some, the memory came back through self-induced hypnotic trances, often during periods of isolation. Many ascended to the mountain tops, which they called heaven to experience it.

Clear memories of the past came through to them. Such happenings of centuries long past, in places they had never known. Some memories were of violence, still others brought peace to the soul.

A quiet tranquility crept into the spirit of all who were blessed with the gift, and more and more men went up into the mountains to find seclusion and pray. These men were called hermits, for they were powerless to share the emotion that had over-taken them.

A DREAM

And once in a dream I looked upwards into a clear, blue-black sky, with an orange moon. I looked upwards into two faces in the clouds, one was a very, old man, the other, a very, old woman. The faces were grieving and full of hopelessness.

I saw an angel in flowing, white robes appear then. He was sitting at a desk with an ancient ink well, and he was writing with a feather, plume pen on an unfurling, white scroll. I could not see the words, but he was tranquil and beautiful, in contrast to the two faces.

The words have never been revealed to me, though somehow, I believe they were this:

"Be not afraid, for after darkness there will be once again be Peace, and the faces of agony will be restored into the countenance of youth, in all of its splendor"

Take Goodness from every story and each interpretation and you will find God.

And during the End Times

I will pour forth my knowledge out over the earth.

THE MOUNTAINS WILL ALWAYS BE THERE

The hour was her very own. In the predawn darkness the black roses were invisible. They were radiant that year. It had been a glorious summer.

Morning came up shyly at first and formed liquid, silver pools over the clouds. Far below the city slept. Mardia let the ocean breeze swill over her face and press the soft fabric of her sari close to her bronze silhouette. She searched the vaporous, grey mist for a lingering star, but they had all vanished. She had magnificent eyes, large, dark, and damp, always damp with excitement, or love, or both.

She thought of Chantal and the first day she had experienced the mountains. She had awakened one morning to discover that their majestic peaks had split open the sky and seemed so close, it was as though she could reach out and touch them. She had trembled and wanted to cry out, but could not speak with the glory of it, and the silent symphony all around was wonderful.

She cried when the last curtain fell during Autumn and hid them once more. It was lonely without the mountains and frightening then.

"They are there little one," Chantal had comforted, "the mountains will always be there."

The sun formed golden pools beneath the pastel clouds and fell in droplets over the snow-white domes of the capital buildings below. It fell upon Mardia and it was warm on her face and bare shoulders.

The mountains were there. She knew that they would always be there.

Shaan found his mother languishing in a chaise surrounded by her flowers.

"Have you ever seen them more brilliant," she marvelled, "so vibrant as this year."

"Don't you say that every year, mother?" He had a wonderful smile and magnificent, dark eyes. Mardia had chosen everything about him and had not been disappointed, not once. The gene bank had doled forth perfection with this one, still, the invisible ceiling of intelligence had not yet been penetrated, as had happened with her only daughter, Allaahna. He had wisdom that was his very own and a great surplus of kindness, but she did not understand why he had always seemed so troubled.

Chantal brought out a silver tray with a china pot of hot tea and a crystal bowl of warm crescents wrapped in a snow-white, linen serviette. Mardia stood and embraced her Ayah but the old woman did not respond, but only bowed and left in silence. She came back in a few minutes with frosted grapes on a pewter platter and perfect, sliced nectarines placed over the leaves.

"We could not live this way without her," said Shaan, frowning deeply.

"Her kind has all but vanished," Mardia agreed.

"She believes in a supreme power," Shaan was fearful.

"Nature is her God, Shaan."

"Still, she has been genetically preserved. Is that natural?"

"I am content with my Ayah. She has extraordinary wisdom."

"Extraordinary, yes, and frightening."

Mardia raised her hand and her son was silenced. He left without partaking in La Petite dejeuner.

He was the first to arrive at the laboratory. He suited up and checked the scanner. The virus was winning.

Down the white corridor, in the operating theatre, Marcael stood alone waiting for the others to arrive. The tables had turned. This day he was the patient. His new heart would be ready in fifteen seconds. The clock on the instrument panel ticked down the moments before surgery. Shareem, the chief surgeon, arrived. The procedure took twelve seconds.

"There," she said casually, "it's done, take care of this one. It should last you another ninety years."

"One hundred," Marcael whispered, the procedure had slightly weakened him.

"Ahe?"

"One hundred," he repeated, "you replaced the other one, one hundred years ago."

"Was that the first replacement?" Shareem smiled.

"Of course," he knew that she was joking with him. At two hundred, he was a vital, healthy specimen. He had been fortunate and he intended to keep it that way. Marcael stood up.

"They are dying like flies now," Shareem said. "We will be needing more cells for the pregnatorium. The bank is nearly depleted."

"Shall I donate?"

"It is up to you, it would help."

"You know that it distresses me to meet up with young clones."

"I can see that your cells are distributed thinly over the entire planet, if you wish."

"How serious is the problem, Shareem?" Marcael asked.

"The virus is winning. It is driving the humots to self-destruct, once infected they cannot control their behavior."

"We cannot expect them to, it is their way of life. We cannot deprive them of pleasure."

"Of course not."

"Let me think about it," Marcael said. "I will let you know soon."

Shareem watched him leave. "I am desperate," she whispered. "What else can be done, nearly all of the donors are moribund, deaths now outnumber fetal creations." She walked to the window and gazed out at the tower, and pondered the most perfect structure on the planet. The yellow sun splashed over its' entirety, making it glare garishly above the domes.

"To think they built that in honor of their God," Shareem shuddered, "what kind of people were the 'ancient ones'?"

It was pleasant outdoors. A soft hum rose up from the ground, which was most soothing to Marcael. His new heart beat regularly as he strolled towards the coastline. Suddenly, the humming stopped. The moment was exhilarating and then the humming resumed once more. Marcael smiled and let the warm sun seep into his pores.

He reached the marble sea wall and walked along the ancient pathway for ten miles, at which point he jumped over the old, stone wall and walked down to meet Celia, at the water's edge.

"Did it go well?" she asked.

"Of course."

"How is Shareem?"

"Agnostic."

"She believes more than she says."

"She is lying then?"

"I suppose. I only know that I caught her praying at the 'Immaculata' just last week."

"The old fool."

"Did the failure effect you this afternoon?", Celia asked him, looking dreamily out over the sea.

"I should say not. I still generate my own energy, I hope, and it is my own heart clone."

"Why did you need the new pump anyway?"

"It was time, that is all."

"How is Aamaan?"

"My great-grandfather is fine, but he has lost nearly twenty of his young sons to the virus."

"Strange isn't it, that only his cells were used at the pregnatorium and so many of his offspring have been stricken."

"They are susceptible because of their behavior," Marcael laughed. "They copulate like worms."

"You mustn't joke, Marcael. They are clones of your grandfather."

"They are not my clones, thanks to my frivolous, promiscuous mother, praise her. She died of natural causes, you know, old age at ninety-seven. Can you believe that. It was the way, she said, in her great-grandmother's time. It was best she said. She would never abandon that notion. It is natural, she would say, we must obey the laws of nature and she was brilliant too, to have died so young."

"Brilliant. I have never heard you speak of her that way. I thought you said she believed in a god of some kind, Sarah's God."

"Yes, still, in many other ways she was brilliant, not scientifically, but in Wisdom."

"Marcael, please, your new heart is distorting your intelligence."

"Perhaps so."

"Anyway, the shut down today caused somewhat of a problem for the humots. The robots outsmarted them into a state of total confusion. It was comical at first, until one of the humots began crying, and the robots could not. It pacified them somehow, the humots that is. They are unpredictable. I worry about them. They still desire to copulate in what they call a natural way and let humans grow and develop in their own bodies. They use the word cherish, they want to cherish one another and the children they produce in this horrible way. The beautiful, black ones are the most stubborn and troublesome. Their genetic strength is more formidable."

"They are magnificent humots sure, still, they are well treated and have been given so much."

"They want freedom."

"They have freedom, they have everything. It is what they all demanded two thousand years ago."

"I fear a revolution."

"You talk like an ancient. You must have cause to revolt."

"I cannot believe I spoke those words."

"Neither can I."

They climbed the wall and walked back to the estate in silence. That night they pleasured each other. Celia requested the device. He took it off and placed it within her body and watched her writhe into a trance. He hated its' power and she was soon unaware of his presence. She was in ecstasy beyond his level. She continued to writhe and finally fell into a deep slumber. He left and did not return.

....

Allaahna left for the village at midnight. Shaan had sufficiently drugged himself and was gently hallucinating. Mardia was asleep in her chambers.

In the village the people waited patiently. When Allaahna arrived, she greeted each one individually. A most, magnificent specimen led her towards the canopy, where the newborn nestled in her mother's arms.

"When did it happen?" Allaahna whispered.

"At daybreak," the young man beamed, "it is female."

"She is perfect then?"

"Yes, in every way."

"This is the beginning, Adahm," Allaahna said softly. "You will be known as the father of Our Savior. She will lead us to the light. She will lead us to God, for after darkness the seed of God will emerge once more."

Beautiful music resounded within the valley and ascended into the heavens and those who were called magnificent raised their voices in praise.

"She is the vessel of life," Adahm rejoiced.

"We are all vessels of life, Adahm," Allaahna spoke softly. "She is the beginning of the new way, the way of nature, the way of God. For the time will come when all women will once again bring forth life from within their own wombs, and heaven will rejoice."

"I am afraid the others will destroy our village if this word gets out. I believe that Shareem is already suspicious. She remembers when natural birth was not an uncommon practice. I believe she still regards it as most beautiful. She denies this in such a desperate way that I must wonder about her sincerity."

"She is vehement about it for sure."

Adahm's eyes widened. Allaahna smiled.

"She believes in the natural superiority of women and she knows not why."

Shareem stared out at the shrine. The word was engraved in marble and the word was Love.

Genetic Memory is love, we must unleash the memory and put it into the brain cells of embryos. It is there, if only it can be tapped. It is trapped now in the millions of cells in every brain.

Allaahna had the gift of genetic memory. Shareem was certain of it. She was also consumed with the idea of unleashing it in her own brain, so that she could pore forth this abundance of knowledge over the earth, so that others might understand as well why they had reached Utopia and yet there was no real happiness, and why now the virus was about to destroy all.

Allaahna was teaching the people of the village. They were all seated. She in the center. The mode was telepathic, her message was received by all.

"The nation that abuses the vessel of life destroys life in all human form. If the vessel of life is to be glorified, all life must be glorified from the beginning unto the end. We are at the beginning of a wondrous new era. We are the conception. With this child a new way has begun."

Allaahna left quietly, the others prayed in silence. They did not notice her departure.

Sarah had just awakened as Allaahna entered the palace. Shaan had already left for the Laboratory.

"Please come in darling," Sarah smiled at her grandaughter.

"Good morning dear," Allaahna drew closer to accept Sarah's outstretched arms.

"Where have you been?" Sarah questioned.

"To the village," Allaahna smiled a little mischievously.

"Ahe," Sarah inhaled slowly, "has it happened?"

"She is beautiful."

"A female," Sarah whispered, the joy in her voice quite beautiful to hear. "Praise God."

"Praise God for all life," Allaahna prayed softly.

Allaahna took her morning bath early. She drew the soft, scented water herself and reprogrammed the robot. Allaahna rejoiced in doing things for herself. She understood the dreams of the humots. "We have needs," they cried out, "needs to create." "The robots do everything better than we can do ourselves. There is no pleasure, no fulfillment in life this way. We are told we must live and live when all we want to do is die. There is no hope for us. We want to create."

The water was warm and soothing, but she could not get her mind off the cries of the humots, it was as though they had hold of her very soul.

"We are given everything and yet we have nothing," they told her to the person. "Given, given, given that is the evil of it all. We are given everything."

"Robots do nothing better," she wanted to cry out. It was heartbreaking, she choked back a sob and reached for her glass and sipped the sweet, cool nectar within it. "They believe I am their savior when I am only one of them. Let me show them the light that is present in every creature of nature," she prayed. "They are full of the light and yet they will not believe it."

Allaahna's thoughts drifted back to the day of her transfiguration. She had been playing near the huge, marble staircase leading up to the shrine of the first Sarah. The sun was brilliant that day, still, the air was cool and dry. She pretended each step was a mountain. She had climbed fifty mountains when it happened. Everything became silent. There was no wind, nothing stirred. The silence was frightening, the sky above was the clearest, deepest blue she had ever known. What happened then had no voice nor image. It was the silence of sensation that took hold of her soul and from that time on nothing in life was ever the same.

She felt the words rather than heard them. The veil of innocent ignorance was forever lifted and she had knowledge. She was knowledge and that knowledge was divine.

"For whenever I pore forth my knowledge upon the earth the end is near."

Allaahna stepped out of her bath and dried herself in the natural way. A white, scented towel slipped off the rack into her waiting arms.

Just a few hundred years ago she, herself, would have been dismembered in her own mother's womb and sucked out after her death. Was the new method really any different?

"Not pre-approved," the words of her brother haunted her.

"Is a soul pre-approved? Can a spirit be dissolved as the embryo. There is no sin, no morality, only pleasures of the body. If pleasure solves all problems, why are the humanots in a pre-revolutionary state, wanting more and more, giving less and less? Why is the virus winning? Will the virus win? The people of the village are pure. If the world discovers them before it is time, humanity as we know it will cease to exist."

Allaahna arrived at the steps of the shrine just as the sun was setting. She prayed until midnight and then headed for the village.

The chanting had already begun. No one noticed her arrival this time, all faces were turned heavenward in prayer and thanksgiving. "This is joy," she whispered. "This is the joy they reject."

"This is the joy the strange beings had found when they landed. They were light years away by now," Allaahna wondered if they could ever return. They also spoke of the light, though they had never returned.

It was nearly midday when she caught up with Shaan at the laboratory.

"It has happened," she confided.

"Allaahna, this is madness," Shaan lowered his voice to an angry whisper. "You will destroy all that science has accomplished. All that has taken nearly two millenniums. We have a Euphoria, this is Utopia. How can your heaven be better than this? We need only desire and our joy is accomplished."

"Joy!!"

"Yes, joy to replace fear and hunger. We have instant transportation to any place on earth through sheer desire."

"Joy!!" Allaahna repeated pensively, "what Joy?"

"There is no hardship, Allaahna," Shaan ignored her quiet sarcasm, "no famine, no poverty, no pestilence, no ....."

"Disease!" she filled in the word, "the virus is winning, Shaan."

"Yes, and you have the divine knowledge to" . . . the word had escaped his lips . . . "You have the knowledge to destroy it and yet you refuse."

"The spread of the disease is one hundred percent preventable," Allaahna said.

"The People must have their pleasure, it is a scientific necessity. Why will you not admit this fact? Pleasure alone makes life worthwhile."

"Pleasure is only physical. Happiness is spiritual. Happiness is eternal."

"Ah, I am fed up with you."

Allaahna knew that he was not. "The virus wishes to rule the planet. Once it enters its' host, it releases toxins that incite unnatural human behavior."

"Allaahna, how dare you! Do you claim viral intelligentsia?"

"Yes, it is so. It will destroy human life as we know it."

"What then?"

"Colonial famine, most of the strain will die out. Some will be frozen in the deepest crevices of the earth. It will only hibernate. It will not die."

"You destroy me, Allaahna, what of science?"

"What of science, science is neutral, it neither controls nor is controllable."

"Allaahna, for nearly one millennium we have been genetically perfect.

"Aren't you forgetting something, brother?"

"The virus?"

"No, the four million pre-born infants used in your scientific experimentation."

"They were not pre-approved. You know that and what can I do about what happened nine hundred years ago?"

"Pre-approved!" Allaahna's voice was barely audible. She did not look at her brother and left in silence. The glaring, yellow lights of the laboratory pierced her brain like icy, razor blades.

Once outside her depression continued. "I am afraid it is too late," she said softly, almost prayerfully to herself. Shaan, her own brother, had said the birth of a child was madness.

The next morning, Shaan confided the worst to his mother. Mardia was shocked.

"The virus is unpredictable," he said somberly. "Unlike the millions destroyed before it, this one has adapted, this one will survive, behavior is its' host."

"Hello! behavior?"

"Yes."

Sarah came in then and embraced both grandson and daughter.

"I have overheard your conversation," she said, "and I am gravely fearful."

"As are we all grandmother," Shaan said. "That is all save Allaahna. No one understands her, grandmother. She is a physicist, author, poet, chemist, mathematician, and even tradesman. She is full of knowledge and gifted in every way and yet she speaks only of love. She says that the universe is only plasma and that each one of us is a universe. Do you believe that she says that each human being is a universe unto itself? No one understands her, grandmother."

"She is a lover, I have known this kind before. Let her teach love, all else will follow," Sarah insisted.

"I am impatient, we must destroy the virus. People are decaying before death. They are on their way to heaven, she says. They are rotting, I say, before our very eyes. They must change their behavior, she says, otherwise no cure will be effective and the virus will win in spite of a cure.

And the child grew in strength, wisdom and in love. At the age of twelve, she entered the city, unbeknownst to Adaam, and she taught from the Immaculata, but the geniuses could not understand, for her wisdom was of the ancient time and in their advancement they had lost the art of determination through dreams and imagination, for they could no longer dream but only exist.

A new mutation of the virus appeared and was more deadly than the first, for it could be inhaled, and it filled the atmosphere and even was carried in the clouds above.

Still, the village was spared through all things natural from conception to the harvesting of grain. And they were pure and clean and knew abundant joy.

In the city, no family among the humanots had been spared and most lay buried in their graves. The aristocrats were stricken, also, for the mutated virus no longer needed behavior to propel it, but rather, only the air they breathed.

There was much wailing and gnashing of teeth, for they had been forewarned by Allaahna that their perverted behavior must cease, but they would not listen.

Sarah and Mardia died peacefully, for it was their choice to forego surgery, knowing that the end was coming and would be horrible. Chantal took her knowledge into the village and soon all were expert tradesmen, who could weave, build, cook, prepare food, grow and preserve. The children were all magnificent born and conceived of the flesh.

The scientific geniuses did everything possible to preserve life, all to no avail.

When the nuclear explosion occurred, the entire surface of the earth was destroyed and its' power descended into the heavens, destroying even the airborne virus in the clouds.

The people of the village were spared. Gradually, each villager was taken up into the light. Sometimes, while two labored in fields together, one would be taken and the other left behind.

They called it the "rapture" and those left behind prayed fervently for their turn to come.

The first Child of God was last to go up into the light.

The earth lingered under ice, in darkness, for one million years.

The child of God slept for one million years.

Slowly, earth was rejuvenated and more wondrous than ever before.

She awakened in paradise in the purest of all innocence, she had but one sadness, she was alone.

Her skin was the color of charred cinder . . . .

EPILOGUE

AN INTERPRETATION
OF
THE DEAD SEA SCROLLS

INTERPRETATION

About fourteen miles east of Jerusalem, near the Dead Sea, a community of Jewish monks was formed. Their life was austere, remote from contemporary Judaism, that had become a most powerful religion, with a strong belief in only one God.

The cult, separating itself from the mother religion, said that "suffering was inseparable from existence, but that inward extinction of the self, and of the senses, culminates in a state of illumination beyond both suffering and existence."

These people delved more and more into the inner universe of the mind, and some found peace there apart from the outer environment, and a very few even felt the embrace of God. Others believed that they were reincarnations of the very ancestors, whose memory cells they had drawn upon. No one understood that we inherit not only the length of our bones and the color of our eyes, but memory as well.

The Hebrews, on the other hand, taught that God made a covenant with a particular people, and to these people he revealed the Torah, the law which they were to obey. They believed that one God existed in the world and cared for all men, and it was out of this love for mankind as a whole, that He taught all men His way of redemption. The Jews believed they were the chosen people of God, and with that blessing came horrendous responsibility.

When this group of Jewish monks separated themselves from contemporary Judaism, they ascended high up into the mountains, which they called heaven, though it was a remote, isolated area, described by one ancient writer as a desolate place, without women, without love, without money.

They tried to go inward into the universe of the mind and spirit, but life was lonely and rewarding only to those who knew the gift, and could call upon the memory of their ancestors. To these men, celibacy became God-like, for they believed that God was alone without woman or wife. They knew, however, that without women the cult would die out, and so therefore, as a matter of necessity, women, (all virgins), were brought into the cult.

Now the high priests were never to marry, nor were they to have any contact with the virgins.

The lower casts of priests were to restrict themselves for as long as possible, remaining with the rest of the monks, obeying all of the laws, dining and bedding down with their fellow men in the barracks.

Those monks who could avoid the virgins were considered of a higher caste, for sexuality had become sinful for them and therefore it was to be avoided, except to procreate.

Joacim, who possessed the gift of ancestral recollection and understood it well, was born into the cult and would have left when he became of age, had not the beautiful Ann been brought into the virgin convent.

The day he saw her first, he was stricken by her beauty. She smiled at him, he was sure of that, and her smile was wonderful.

He had always hated the demands of celibacy made by the high priests, and knew from an early age the stupidity of them. In memory, he knew well the purity of consummation through the very first parents. Because of his gift he had discarded the story of Eden, a snake devil, and a merciless God. What fool, he often wondered, had fanaticized this fictional joke upon the Hebrews. Still, he was born into the cult and was determined to live by its rules, until he came of age, which would be in less than three months.

Ann smiled at him frequently in the months to follow. Still, she made no move to contact him, which was the way.

She was dark and beautiful, perhaps Ethiopian of origin, he thought. Her mouth was soft and sensuous, and her eyes the deepest he had ever seen. He lingered too long one day to gaze into them, as they both stood by the spring-fed well, and was disciplined by the high priest.

Joacim was often disciplined. It was a simple ritual. He would be shunned and not allowed to participate in the sacred meal with the high priests for a designated time. He enjoyed the solitude, for although the food was much plainer, the wine was fermented and so much better than the fresh wine served to the high priests.

He supped the fermented wine and could not dismiss the vision of Ann by the fountain from his mind. He knew he must approach her, but he was young and uncertain, and he knew she would be shy.

For many days he lingered on the dunes near the convent and finally one day she passed by. When he smiled, she lowered her eyes and it was then that he knew somehow he must have her. He would approach the high priest for permission.

Their love was immediate and a child was conceived. When sufficient time had passed according to the rules, they were married, and Joacim, because he was a married man, was reduced to a lower level in the caste, and was thereafter more or less ignored by the Holy High Priest.

They had only one child, a girl, who they called Mary, after Maara, the ancestor of Joacim. The one who had first seen the light, and the one whose memory cells he contained in the universe of his brain.

The family stayed with the cult and were comfortable in their own happiness apart from the rest, still obeying their rules.

At the age of twelve, Mary was taken into the convent of the virgins, and only allowed visits to the domain of her parents on special occasions, such as the holy feast of Passover or Honnika.

Mary slipped away to her parents far more often than was permitted, but no one noticed, for the virgins were not so strictly scrutinized as were the young priests.

A VERSION
OF THE
GREATEST STORY EVER TOLD

And from out of this desolate place two brothers or cousins came forth. One rigidly obeyed the rules of the cult and believed the word of the Torah to be sacred. He was called just. The other, who had the gift of memory, realized the foolishness of the early beliefs, and he was called misguided or the wayward priest.

This man had been born of a virgin, that is he had been conceived before the required time of courtship, by a priest and a virgin. According to the rules of the cult, a maiden was still called a virgin until after marriage, even though she became pregnant first. Though this was frowned upon, it was still within the law, unless the virgin became pregnant by one outside of the cult and not her betrothed. In such a case, by law she could be stoned to death at the gates of the city.

The mother of the wayward priest had run into this difficulty when she became pregnant not by her betrothed. At first, her betrothed, who was of a royal family, decided to save her life by simply declaring a divorce. In this way the maiden would be scorned and her child declared an unfortunate, but at least her life would be spared.

It is said that afterwards, when he decided that the child might indeed be his own, they were married. After the birth of the wayward priest they had three other sons and two daughters.

This priest remained within the cult for thirty years and remained celibate, but he was far from close to his family and one day he left them all forever.

He knew, because of his gift, that the stories of the Torah were foolish and fictional and even how and why they came to exist, but He knew also that the people would not understand his explanation and might very well stone him to death for blasphemy, if he attempted to tell them the truth.

He decided to simply preach a gospel of love and take this word forth to the people.

It was during this time that he was declared the evil priest and labelled irreverent.

At a wedding feast, where sweet wine was served as was the custom, he had his followers fill the emptied wine vats with fermented wine, which he referred to as water. The guests became slightly intoxicated and believed this to be a kind of magic. He had only given up his own wine at the request of his mother, still, the story of his magic went forth and his followers became great.

He preached not the word of the Torah, but the word of love, which was the first human emotion on earth, and he learned to feel it even as the first woman had, for it was all contained there in the cells of his memory.

His enemies called him a wine briber, a womanizer, and a blasphemer, and he dared to defy them all.

Now, when the high priest of the cult went out to bless the fishermen, and their ships, as they brought in the catch, he did not walk through the waters as did the others, but rather walked out on a wooden built pier, made especially for him and no one else. This custom was referred to as walking on water.

One evening, as the ships approached after a treacherous storm, the high priest, fearful of the elements, did not appear but stayed atop the mountain.

The wayward priest, himself, met the ships and walked out on the dock to greet them. As he did so the wind changed and the seas became calm once again, and the fishermen said; "look, he walks upon water and calms the seas." With that, twelve of the men left family and the assinian cult and began to follow the wayward priest. They journeyed throughout the land spreading the word of love, goodness, and the story of the one true God.

Many things went unexplained. He saved a man from bleeding to death by applying pressure to his wound, and they said it was a miracle and called his hands blessed.

He soothed a boy, who was experiencing an epileptic seizure, and taught him how to tell when one was about to commence, by recognizing an aura, and to take hiding in some safe place. The people said that the boy had been possessed, and the wayward priest had exorcized him.

At one place, he brought a feverish child out of a coma, by using cool compacts and they said that he had brought her back from the dead.

The word of the miracles spread to all regions, and as much as the wise one tried to explain them, the people cried out that he was the son of God.

Though he was not himself of priestly birth, he wore the white robes of the high priests to symbolize to the people that every human is a priest before God.

He lashed out at the money changers in the temple, and also at the very idea of the paying of coins to atone for sin. For he preached that sin could only be forgiven through grace and goodness towards one's fellow man.

He taught that:

The mother who gives of her life unconditionally in the love of her child is an ordinary thing of beauty.

The mother who gives unconditional love to all children is the rarest of inspirations for humanity.

He stood high atop the mountainside and the misty clouds fell like a soft, holy vestment over his silhouette. As the sunset he turned to the others kneeling below and His transfiguration into radiance filled them with awe.

"My Lord and My God" they cried out, but He rebuked them and they were scorned.

"It is only the sunset," he rebuked them, "how easily you are tricked."

And the next year on the same day, at the same hour, He repeated the ritual. There were twelve others present and once again the transfiguration took place. His radiance was blinding, but the light came through Him into their souls and brought peace, and they said he was the son of God. He replied, "all children are the children of God." They called him Blessed, but rather he said; "Blessed be God.

Blessed be His Holy name.

Blessed are the pure of heart, for theirs is the Kingdom of Heaven.

Blessed are the merciful, for they shall obtain mercy.

Blessed are they that hunger and thirst after
justice, for they shall have their fill.

Blessed are they that mourn, for they shall be comforted.

Blessed are the meek, for they shall possess the land.

Blessed are they that suffer persecution for
justice' sake, for they shall see God.

And some people there found intimacy with God and experienced wonderful things, that came from within their own universe and not from without, and the wayward priest smiled upon them and blessed them.

Many of these people were heretofore dying of catastrophic wounding from injuries of birth or other accidental traumas. Others had bodies that were being overtaken by cancers and viral afflictions. They were miraculously cured from within through their very own union with God.

It was during this time that fearful men became full of awe, and the word was spread that this man was truly the son of God. "We are all the sons of God", he cried out. "I am the light, I am the truth, I am the Word", and his wisdom spread to every corner of the world.

He changed many things about the ancient religion. He cancelled the sacrificial slaughter of the lamb and gave himself. "I am the lamb of God", he said, "who takes away the sins of the world." He continued the ritual using only bread and wine saying, "this is my body, this is my blood, do this often in memory of me."

They crucified him then and the members of his cult, the Assinians, felt sorry and ashamed, for they too had called him blasphemous.

At dusk, that day, they took him down from the cross and laid him to rest in a tomb that was comfortable. The Assinians, who believed that certain people were reincarnations of angels and saints, (indeed, it was believed that the natural father of the wayward priest was himself the holy spirit, and his son therefore was believed to have been conceived of the holy spirit), sent one of these reincarnated angels to guard his tomb. When, the second day after the crucifixion, the woman came to the tomb to pray, this angel informed her that he had been taken up into the hilltop home of the highest priest, which they called heaven.

He spoke to his followers only one time after that to reassure the doubter, but after that, until his death, lived in the heaven of the highest priest and was called the holy of Holies.

For two thousand years the word spread, and though evil prevailed, at times goodness thrived, through the meek and the merciful, the pure of heart, those that mourned, those that suffered persecution for justice sake, and those that hungered and thirsted for righteousness.

And two thousand years after the coming of the Messiah who brought only love to mankind; The planet once more was threatened

God poured forth His knowledge upon Earth, until the minds of His people swelled with an intelligence that was once again wondrous, and great and powerful things were accomplished beyond imagination

The appearance of evil began to once again seep up from the darkness.

Will a new leader emerge. One filled with the goodness of God

Let us pray

CPSIA information can be obtained
at www.ICGtesting.com
Printed in the USA
FFOW04n1225230414
4970FF